Apophis's Daily Gratitude Journal

Matthew Petchinsky

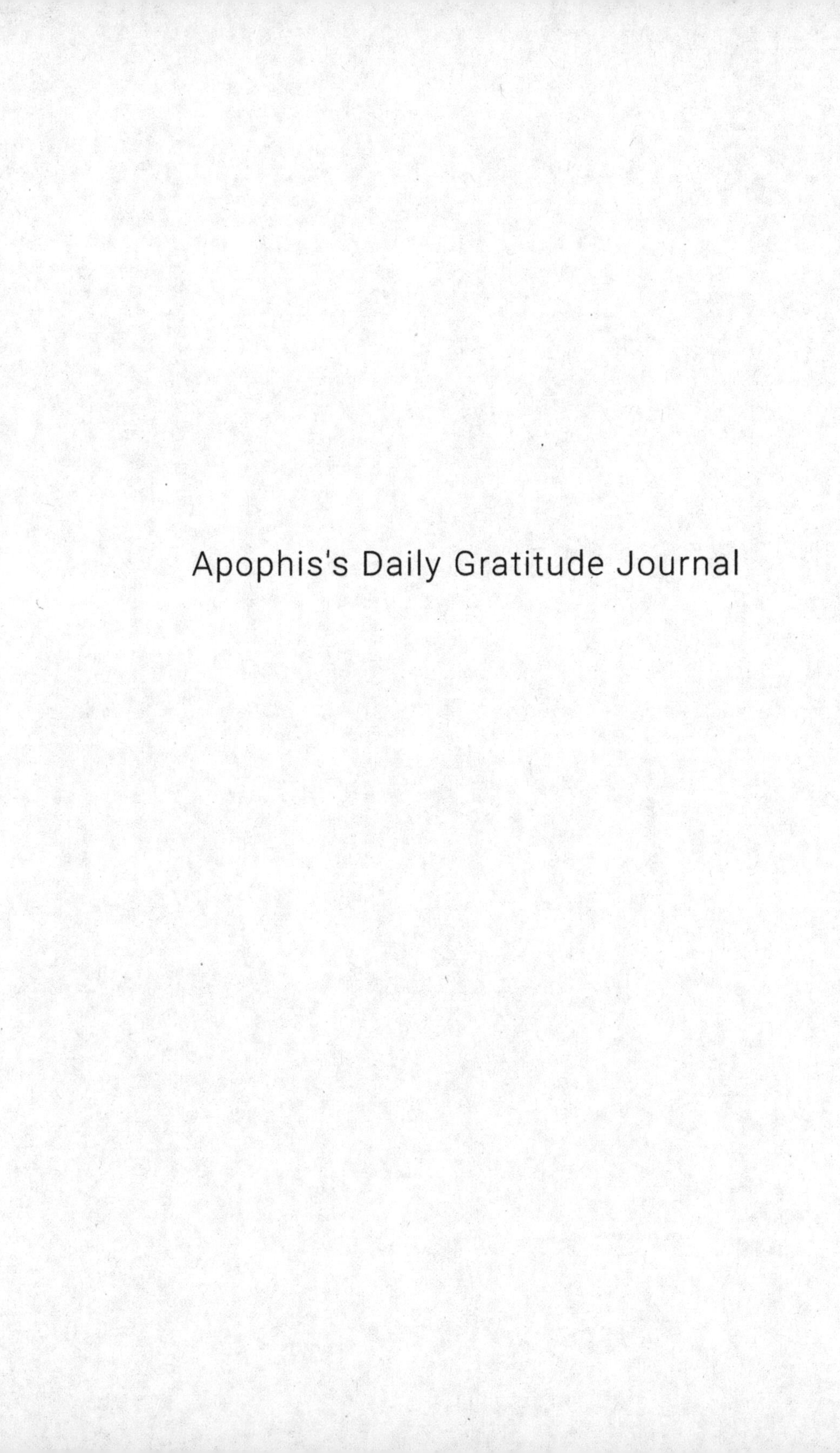

Apophis's Daily Gratitude Journal

Apophis's Daily Gratitude Journal
By Matthew Petchinsky

Instructions for Using Your Gratitude Journal
Daily Use
Morning Reflection:

- Start your day with a positive mindset by reflecting on three things you are grateful for. These can be simple pleasures or significant aspects of your life.
- Write down a positive affirmation to set the tone for your day. This could be a statement that motivates you or reinforces a positive belief.
- Plan one action or intention to make your day great. This helps you focus on something positive you can control.

Afternoon Check-in:

- Take a moment during your midday break to reflect on a positive moment from the morning. This helps reinforce positive experiences.
- Write down something you have accomplished, no matter how small. This builds a sense of achievement and progress.

Evening Reflection:

- At the end of your day, list three things that made you happy. This practice helps you end the day on a positive note.
- Reflect on someone you are grateful for and why. This fosters appreciation and strengthens relationships.
- Write down something you learned today. It could be a new fact, a life lesson, or an insight about yourself.
- Circle your feelings from the day. This helps you become more aware of your emotions and patterns.

Nightly Reflection:

- Before bed, list three things you are grateful for. This helps you end your day with gratitude and positivity.
- Reflect on what could have made your day better. This isn't to dwell on negatives but to consider areas for improvement.
- Note something you are looking forward to tomorrow. This creates anticipation and a positive outlook for the next day.

Weekly Use
Weekly Summary:

- At the end of each week, reflect on the highlight of your week. This helps you remember and cherish positive experiences.
- List three things you are grateful for from the past week. This practice reinforces the habit of gratitude.
- Reflect on one thing you learned this week. This promotes continuous learning and growth.
- Set goals for the next week. This keeps you focused and motivated.

Monthly Use
Monthly Reflection:

- At the end of each month, think about the highlight of your month. This helps you appreciate significant moments.
- List three things you are grateful for from the past month. This reinforces gratitude on a larger scale.
- Reflect on one significant accomplishment. This builds a sense of achievement and progress.
- Write down something you are looking forward to in the next month. This helps you maintain a positive outlook.

Additional Notes

- Use the notes section to jot down any additional thoughts, reflections, or ideas that come to mind throughout your journaling process.

Tips for Success:

- Be consistent. Try to use your journal every day to build a strong habit.
- Be honest and authentic. Write down what you truly feel and experience.
- Take your time. Allow yourself a few quiet moments to reflect and write.
- Review past entries. Occasionally look back at previous entries to see your progress and recurring themes of gratitude.

By following these instructions and using your gratitude journal regularly, you can cultivate a positive mindset, enhance your well-being, and develop a deeper appreciation for the good things in your life.

Date: ___________________________(Day 1)
Morning Reflection
Three things I am grateful for today:

Positive affirmation for today:

What can I do today to make it a great day?

Afternoon Check-in
A positive moment from the morning:

Something I accomplished today:

Evening Reflection
Three things that made me happy today:

Someone I am grateful for today and why:

Something I learned today:

How I felt today (circle all that apply):

- Happy
- Excited
- Content
- Relaxed
- Anxious
- Stressed
- Other: _______________________________

Nightly Reflection
Three things I am grateful for before going to bed:

What could have made today better?

One thing I am looking forward to tomorrow:

Date: ________________________(Day 2)
Morning Reflection
Three things I am grateful for today:

Positive affirmation for today:

What can I do today to make it a great day?

Afternoon Check-in
A positive moment from the morning:

Something I accomplished today:

Evening Reflection
Three things that made me happy today:

Someone I am grateful for today and why:

Something I learned today:

How I felt today (circle all that apply):

- ∘ Happy
- ∘ Excited
- ∘ Content
- ∘ Relaxed
- ∘ Anxious
- ∘ Stressed
- ∘ Other: _________________

Nightly Reflection
Three things I am grateful for before going to bed:

What could have made today better?

One thing I am looking forward to tomorrow:

Date: _______________________(Day 3)
Morning Reflection
Three things I am grateful for today:

Positive affirmation for today:

What can I do today to make it a great day?

Afternoon Check-in
A positive moment from the morning:

Something I accomplished today:

Evening Reflection
Three things that made me happy today:

Someone I am grateful for today and why:

Something I learned today:

How I felt today (circle all that apply):

- Happy
- Excited
- Content
- Relaxed
- Anxious
- Stressed
- Other: _________________

Nightly Reflection
Three things I am grateful for before going to bed:

What could have made today better?

One thing I am looking forward to tomorrow:

Date: _______________________(Day 4)
Morning Reflection
Three things I am grateful for today:

Positive affirmation for today:

What can I do today to make it a great day?

Afternoon Check-in
A positive moment from the morning:

Something I accomplished today:

Evening Reflection
Three things that made me happy today:

Someone I am grateful for today and why:

Something I learned today:

How I felt today (circle all that apply):

- Happy
- Excited
- Content
- Relaxed
- Anxious
- Stressed
- Other: ______________

Nightly Reflection
Three things I am grateful for before going to bed:

What could have made today better?

One thing I am looking forward to tomorrow:

Date: _________________________(Day 5)
Morning Reflection
Three things I am grateful for today:

Positive affirmation for today:

What can I do today to make it a great day?

Afternoon Check-in
A positive moment from the morning:

Something I accomplished today:

Evening Reflection
Three things that made me happy today:

Someone I am grateful for today and why:

Something I learned today:

How I felt today (circle all that apply):

- Happy
- Excited
- Content
- Relaxed
- Anxious
- Stressed
- Other: ________________

Nightly Reflection
Three things I am grateful for before going to bed:

What could have made today better?

One thing I am looking forward to tomorrow:

Date: ________________________(Day 6)
Morning Reflection
Three things I am grateful for today:

Positive affirmation for today:

What can I do today to make it a great day?

Afternoon Check-in
A positive moment from the morning:

Something I accomplished today:

Evening Reflection
Three things that made me happy today:

Someone I am grateful for today and why:

Something I learned today:

How I felt today (circle all that apply):

- Happy
- Excited
- Content
- Relaxed
- Anxious
- Stressed
- Other: _______________

Nightly Reflection
Three things I am grateful for before going to bed:

What could have made today better?

One thing I am looking forward to tomorrow:

Date: _________________________________(Day 7)
Morning Reflection
Three things I am grateful for today:

Positive affirmation for today:

What can I do today to make it a great day?

Afternoon Check-in

A positive moment from the morning:

Something I accomplished today:

Evening Reflection
Three things that made me happy today:

Someone I am grateful for today and why:

Something I learned today:

How I felt today (circle all that apply):

- ◦ Happy
- ◦ Excited
- ◦ Content
- ◦ Relaxed
- ◦ Anxious
- ◦ Stressed
- ◦ Other: _______________

Nightly Reflection
Three things I am grateful for before going to bed:

What could have made today better?

One thing I am looking forward to tomorrow:

<u>**Week 1 Summery**</u>
Weekly Summary (to be filled out at the end of the week)
The highlight of my week:

Three things I am grateful for this week:

One thing I learned this week:

Goals for next week:

Date: ________________________(Day 8)
Morning Reflection
Three things I am grateful for today:

Positive affirmation for today:

What can I do today to make it a great day?

Afternoon Check-in
A positive moment from the morning:

Something I accomplished today:

Evening Reflection
Three things that made me happy today:

Someone I am grateful for today and why:

Something I learned today:

How I felt today (circle all that apply):

- Happy
- Excited
- Content
- Relaxed
- Anxious
- Stressed
- Other: _________________

Nightly Reflection
Three things I am grateful for before going to bed:

What could have made today better?

One thing I am looking forward to tomorrow:

Date: _______________________(Day 9)
Morning Reflection
Three things I am grateful for today:

Positive affirmation for today:

What can I do today to make it a great day?

Afternoon Check-in
A positive moment from the morning:

Something I accomplished today:

Evening Reflection
Three things that made me happy today:

Someone I am grateful for today and why:

Something I learned today:

How I felt today (circle all that apply):

- Happy
- Excited
- Content
- Relaxed
- Anxious
- Stressed
- Other: ___________________

Nightly Reflection
Three things I am grateful for before going to bed:

What could have made today better?

One thing I am looking forward to tomorrow:

Date: _______________________(Day 10)
Morning Reflection
Three things I am grateful for today:

Positive affirmation for today:

What can I do today to make it a great day?

Afternoon Check-in
A positive moment from the morning:

Something I accomplished today:

Evening Reflection
Three things that made me happy today:

Someone I am grateful for today and why:

Something I learned today:

How I felt today (circle all that apply):

- Happy
- Excited
- Content
- Relaxed
- Anxious
- Stressed
- Other: _______________

Nightly Reflection
Three things I am grateful for before going to bed:

What could have made today better?

One thing I am looking forward to tomorrow:

Date: _______________________(Day 11)
Morning Reflection
Three things I am grateful for today:

Positive affirmation for today:

What can I do today to make it a great day?

Afternoon Check-in
A positive moment from the morning:

Something I accomplished today:

Evening Reflection
Three things that made me happy today:

Someone I am grateful for today and why:

Something I learned today:

How I felt today (circle all that apply):

- Happy
- Excited
- Content
- Relaxed
- Anxious
- Stressed
- Other: _______________

Nightly Reflection
Three things I am grateful for before going to bed:

What could have made today better?

One thing I am looking forward to tomorrow:

Date: ________________________(Day 12)
Morning Reflection
Three things I am grateful for today:

Positive affirmation for today:

What can I do today to make it a great day?

Afternoon Check-in
A positive moment from the morning:

Something I accomplished today:

Evening Reflection
Three things that made me happy today:

Someone I am grateful for today and why:

Something I learned today:

How I felt today (circle all that apply):

- ° Happy
- ° Excited
- ° Content
- ° Relaxed
- ° Anxious
- ° Stressed
- ° Other: _________________

Nightly Reflection
Three things I am grateful for before going to bed:

What could have made today better?

One thing I am looking forward to tomorrow:

Date: _______________________________(Day 13)
Morning Reflection
Three things I am grateful for today:

Positive affirmation for today:

What can I do today to make it a great day?

Afternoon Check-in
A positive moment from the morning:

Something I accomplished today:

Evening Reflection
Three things that made me happy today:

Someone I am grateful for today and why:

Something I learned today:

How I felt today (circle all that apply):

- Happy
- Excited
- Content
- Relaxed
- Anxious
- Stressed
- Other: _______________

Nightly Reflection
Three things I am grateful for before going to bed:

What could have made today better?

One thing I am looking forward to tomorrow:

Date: _______________________(Day 14)
Morning Reflection
Three things I am grateful for today:

Positive affirmation for today:

What can I do today to make it a great day?

Afternoon Check-in
A positive moment from the morning:

Something I accomplished today:

Evening Reflection
Three things that made me happy today:

Someone I am grateful for today and why:

Something I learned today:

How I felt today (circle all that apply):

- Happy
- Excited
- Content
- Relaxed
- Anxious
- Stressed
- Other: ________________

Nightly Reflection
Three things I am grateful for before going to bed:

What could have made today better?

One thing I am looking forward to tomorrow:

<u>**Week 2 Summery**</u>
Weekly Summary (to be filled out at the end of the week)
The highlight of my week:

Three things I am grateful for this week:

One thing I learned this week:

**Goals for next week:

Date: _______________________(Day 15)
Morning Reflection
Three things I am grateful for today:

Positive affirmation for today:

What can I do today to make it a great day?

Afternoon Check-in

A positive moment from the morning:

Something I accomplished today:

Evening Reflection
Three things that made me happy today:

Someone I am grateful for today and why:

Something I learned today:

How I felt today (circle all that apply):

- Happy
- Excited
- Content
- Relaxed
- Anxious
- Stressed
- Other: _______________

Nightly Reflection
Three things I am grateful for before going to bed:

What could have made today better?

One thing I am looking forward to tomorrow:

Date: ___________________________(Day 16)
Morning Reflection
Three things I am grateful for today:

Positive affirmation for today:

What can I do today to make it a great day?

Afternoon Check-in

A positive moment from the morning:

Something I accomplished today:

Evening Reflection
Three things that made me happy today:

Someone I am grateful for today and why:

Something I learned today:

How I felt today (circle all that apply):

- Happy
- Excited
- Content
- Relaxed
- Anxious
- Stressed
- Other: _______________

Nightly Reflection
Three things I am grateful for before going to bed:

What could have made today better?

One thing I am looking forward to tomorrow:

Date: _______________________(Day 17)
Morning Reflection
Three things I am grateful for today:

Positive affirmation for today:

What can I do today to make it a great day?

Afternoon Check-in

A positive moment from the morning:

Something I accomplished today:

Evening Reflection
Three things that made me happy today:

Someone I am grateful for today and why:

Something I learned today:

How I felt today (circle all that apply):

- Happy
- Excited
- Content
- Relaxed
- Anxious
- Stressed
- Other: _________________

Nightly Reflection
Three things I am grateful for before going to bed:

What could have made today better?

One thing I am looking forward to tomorrow:

Date: _______________________________(Day 18)
Morning Reflection
Three things I am grateful for today:

Positive affirmation for today:

What can I do today to make it a great day?

Afternoon Check-in
A positive moment from the morning:

Something I accomplished today:

Evening Reflection
Three things that made me happy today:

Someone I am grateful for today and why:

Something I learned today:

How I felt today (circle all that apply):

- Happy
- Excited
- Content
- Relaxed
- Anxious
- Stressed
- Other: _______________

Nightly Reflection
Three things I am grateful for before going to bed:

What could have made today better?

One thing I am looking forward to tomorrow:

Date: ________________________(Day 19)
Morning Reflection
Three things I am grateful for today:

Positive affirmation for today:

What can I do today to make it a great day?

Afternoon Check-in
A positive moment from the morning:

Something I accomplished today:

Evening Reflection
Three things that made me happy today:

Someone I am grateful for today and why:

Something I learned today:

How I felt today (circle all that apply):

- Happy
- Excited
- Content
- Relaxed
- Anxious
- Stressed
- Other: _________________

Nightly Reflection
Three things I am grateful for before going to bed:

What could have made today better?

One thing I am looking forward to tomorrow:

Date: _______________________________(Day 20)
Morning Reflection
Three things I am grateful for today:

Positive affirmation for today:

What can I do today to make it a great day?

Afternoon Check-in
A positive moment from the morning:

Something I accomplished today:

Evening Reflection
Three things that made me happy today:

Someone I am grateful for today and why:

Something I learned today:

How I felt today (circle all that apply):

- ° Happy
- ° Excited
- ° Content
- ° Relaxed
- ° Anxious
- ° Stressed
- ° Other: ______________________

Nightly Reflection
Three things I am grateful for before going to bed:

What could have made today better?

One thing I am looking forward to tomorrow:

Date: ________________________(Day 21)
Morning Reflection
Three things I am grateful for today:

Positive affirmation for today:

What can I do today to make it a great day?

Afternoon Check-in
A positive moment from the morning:

Something I accomplished today:

Evening Reflection
Three things that made me happy today:

Someone I am grateful for today and why:

Something I learned today:

How I felt today (circle all that apply):

- Happy
- Excited
- Content
- Relaxed
- Anxious
- Stressed
- Other: _______________

Nightly Reflection
Three things I am grateful for before going to bed:

What could have made today better?

One thing I am looking forward to tomorrow:

<u>Week 3 Summary Review</u>
Weekly Summary (to be filled out at the end of the week)
The highlight of my week:

Three things I am grateful for this week:

One thing I learned this week:

Goals for next week:

Date: _______________________(Day 22)
Morning Reflection
Three things I am grateful for today:

Positive affirmation for today:

What can I do today to make it a great day?

Afternoon Check-in
A positive moment from the morning:

Something I accomplished today:

Evening Reflection
Three things that made me happy today:

Someone I am grateful for today and why:

Something I learned today:

How I felt today (circle all that apply):

- Happy
- Excited
- Content
- Relaxed
- Anxious
- Stressed
- Other: _______________

Nightly Reflection
Three things I am grateful for before going to bed:

What could have made today better?

One thing I am looking forward to tomorrow:

Date: _______________________(Day 23)
Morning Reflection
Three things I am grateful for today:

Positive affirmation for today:

What can I do today to make it a great day?

Afternoon Check-in
A positive moment from the morning:

Something I accomplished today:

Evening Reflection
Three things that made me happy today:

Someone I am grateful for today and why:

Something I learned today:

How I felt today (circle all that apply):

- ◦ Happy
- ◦ Excited
- ◦ Content
- ◦ Relaxed
- ◦ Anxious
- ◦ Stressed
- ◦ Other: _______________

Nightly Reflection
Three things I am grateful for before going to bed:

What could have made today better?

One thing I am looking forward to tomorrow:

Date: _________________________(Day 24)
Morning Reflection
Three things I am grateful for today:

Positive affirmation for today:

What can I do today to make it a great day?

Afternoon Check-in
A positive moment from the morning:

Something I accomplished today:

Evening Reflection
Three things that made me happy today:

Someone I am grateful for today and why:

Something I learned today:

How I felt today (circle all that apply):

- ◦ Happy
- ◦ Excited
- ◦ Content
- ◦ Relaxed
- ◦ Anxious
- ◦ Stressed
- ◦ Other: _________________

Nightly Reflection
Three things I am grateful for before going to bed:

What could have made today better?

One thing I am looking forward to tomorrow:

Date: _______________________________(Day 25)
Morning Reflection
Three things I am grateful for today:

Positive affirmation for today:

What can I do today to make it a great day?

Afternoon Check-in

A positive moment from the morning:

Something I accomplished today:

Evening Reflection
Three things that made me happy today:

Someone I am grateful for today and why:

Something I learned today:

How I felt today (circle all that apply):

- Happy
- Excited
- Content
- Relaxed
- Anxious
- Stressed
- Other: _________________

Nightly Reflection
Three things I am grateful for before going to bed:

What could have made today better?

One thing I am looking forward to tomorrow:

Date: _______________________________(Day 26)
Morning Reflection
Three things I am grateful for today:

What can I do today to make it a great day?

Afternoon Check-in
A positive moment from the morning:

Something I accomplished today:

Evening Reflection
Three things that made me happy today:

Someone I am grateful for today and why:

Something I learned today:

How I felt today (circle all that apply):

- ° Happy
- ° Excited
- ° Content
- ° Relaxed
- ° Anxious
- ° Stressed
- ° Other: _______________

Nightly Reflection
Three things I am grateful for before going to bed:

What could have made today better?

One thing I am looking forward to tomorrow:

Date: _______________________(Day 27)
Morning Reflection
Three things I am grateful for today:

Positive affirmation for today:

What can I do today to make it a great day?

Afternoon Check-in
A positive moment from the morning:

Something I accomplished today:

Evening Reflection
Three things that made me happy today:

Someone I am grateful for today and why:

Something I learned today:

How I felt today (circle all that apply):

- Happy
- Excited
- Content
- Relaxed
- Anxious
- Stressed
- Other: _________________

Nightly Reflection
Three things I am grateful for before going to bed:

What could have made today better?

One thing I am looking forward to tomorrow:

Date: _______________________(Day 28)
Morning Reflection
Three things I am grateful for today:

Positive affirmation for today:

What can I do today to make it a great day?

Afternoon Check-in
A positive moment from the morning:

Something I accomplished today:

Evening Reflection
Three things that made me happy today:

Someone I am grateful for today and why:

Something I learned today:

How I felt today (circle all that apply):

- Happy
- Excited
- Content
- Relaxed
- Anxious
- Stressed
- Other: ___________________

Nightly Reflection
Three things I am grateful for before going to bed:

What could have made today better?

One thing I am looking forward to tomorrow:

<u>**Week 4 summary review**</u>
Weekly Summary (to be filled out at the end of the week)
The highlight of my week:

Three things I am grateful for this week:

One thing I learned this week:

Goals for next week:

Date: _______________________(Day 29)
Morning Reflection
Three things I am grateful for today:

Positive affirmation for today:

What can I do today to make it a great day?

Afternoon Check-in

A positive moment from the morning:

Something I accomplished today:

Evening Reflection
Three things that made me happy today:

Someone I am grateful for today and why:

Something I learned today:

How I felt today (circle all that apply):

- Happy
- Excited
- Content
- Relaxed
- Anxious
- Stressed
- Other: _______________

Nightly Reflection
Three things I am grateful for before going to bed:

What could have made today better?

One thing I am looking forward to tomorrow:

Date: _______________________(Day 30)
Morning Reflection
Three things I am grateful for today:

Positive affirmation for today:

What can I do today to make it a great day?

Afternoon Check-in
A positive moment from the morning:

Something I accomplished today:

Evening Reflection
Three things that made me happy today:

Someone I am grateful for today and why:

Something I learned today:

How I felt today (circle all that apply):

- Happy
- Excited
- Content
- Relaxed
- Anxious
- Stressed
- Other: _______________

Nightly Reflection
Three things I am grateful for before going to bed:

What could have made today better?

One thing I am looking forward to tomorrow:

Date: ___________________________(Day 31)
Morning Reflection
Three things I am grateful for today:

Positive affirmation for today:

What can I do today to make it a great day?

Afternoon Check-in

A positive moment from the morning:

Something I accomplished today:

Evening Reflection
Three things that made me happy today:

Someone I am grateful for today and why:

Something I learned today:

How I felt today (circle all that apply):

- Happy
- Excited
- Content
- Relaxed
- Anxious
- Stressed
- Other: _______________

Nightly Reflection
Three things I am grateful for before going to bed:

What could have made today better?

One thing I am looking forward to tomorrow:

Monthly Reflection (to be filled out at the end of the month)
The highlight of my month:

Six things I am grateful for this month:

One thing I accomplished this month:

things I am looking forward to next month:

Notes: These notes are to reflect of your experience with this gratitude journal.

<u>Message from the Author:</u>

I hope you enjoyed this book, I love astrology and knew there was not a book such as this out on the shelf. I love metaphysical items as well. Please check out my other books:

-Life of Government Benefits

-My life of Hell

-My life with Hydrocephalus

-Red Sky

-World Domination:Woman's rule

-World Domination:Woman's Rule 2: The War

-Life and Banishment of Apophis: book 1

-The Kidney Friendly Diet

-The Ultimate Hemp Cookbook

-Creating a Dispensary(legally)

-Cleanliness throughout life: the importance of showering from childhood to adulthood.

-Strong Roots: The Risks of Overcoddling children

-Hemp Horoscopes: Cosmic Insights and Earthly Healing

- Celestial Hemp Navigating the Zodiac: Through the Green Cosmos

-Astrological Hemp: Aligning The Stars with Earth's Ancient Herb

-The Astrological Guide to Hemp: Stars, Signs, and Sacred Leaves

-Green Growth: Innovative Marketing Strategies for your Hemp Products and Dispensary

-Cosmic Cannabis

-Astrological Munchies

-Henry The Hemp

-Zodiacal Roots: The Astrological Soul Of Hemp

- **Green Constellations: Intersection of Hemp and Zodiac**

-Hemp in The Houses: An astrological Adventure Through The Cannabis Galaxy

-Galactic Ganja Guide

Heavenly Hemp

Zodiac Leaves

Doctor Who Astrology

Cannastrology

Stellar Satvias and Cosmic Indicas

<u>Celestial Cannabis: A Zodiac Journey</u>

AstroHerbology: The Sky and The Soil: Volume 1

AstroHerbology:Celestial Cannabis:Volume 2

Cosmic Cannabis Cultivation

The Starry Guide to Herbal Harmony: Volume 1

The Starry Guide to Herbal Harmony: Cannabis Universe: Volume 2

Yugioh Astrology: Astrological Guide to Deck, Duels and more

Nightmare Mansion: Echoes of The Abyss

Nightmare Mansion 2: Legacy of Shadows

Nightmare Mansion 3: Shadows of the Forgotten

Nightmare Mansion 4: Echoes of the Damned

The Life and Banishment of Apophis: Book 2

Nightmare Mansion: Halls of Despair

<u>Healing with Herb: Cannabis and Hydrocephalus</u>

<u>Planetary Pot: Aligning with Astrological Herbs: Volume 1</u>

Fast Track to Freedom: 30 Days to Financial Independence Using AI, Assets, and Agile Hustles

<u>Cosmic Hemp Pathways</u>

How to Become Financially Free in 30 Days: 10,000 Paths to Prosperity

Zodiacal Herbage: Astrological Insights: Volume 1

Nightmare Mansion: Whispers in the Walls

The Daleks Invade Atlantis

Henry the hemp and Hydrocephalus

10X The Kidney Friendly Diet

Cannabis Universe: Adult coloring book

Hemp Astrology: The Healing Power of the Stars

Zodiacal Herbage: Astrological Insights: Cannabis Universe: Volume 2

<u>**Planetary Pot: Aligning with Astrological Herbs: Cannabis Universes: Volume 2**</u>

Doctor Who Meets the Replicators and SG-1: The Ultimate Battle for Survival

Nightmare Mansion: Curse of the Blood Moon

<u>**The Celestial Stoner: A Guide to the Zodiac**</u>

Cosmic Pleasures: Sex Toy Astrology for Every Sign

Hydrocephalus Astrology: Navigating the Stars and Healing Waters

Lapis and the Mischievous Chocolate Bar

Celestial Positions: Sexual Astrology for Every Sign

Apophis's Shadow Work Journal: : A Journey of Self-Discovery and Healing

Kinky Cosmos: Sexual Kink Astrology for Every Sign

Digital Cosmos: The Astrological Digimon Compendium

Stellar Seeds: The Cosmic Guide to Growing with Astrology

If you want solar for your home go here: https://www.harborso-lar.live/apophisenterprises/

Get Some Tarot cards: https://www.makeplayingcards.com/sell/apophis-occult-shop

Get some shirts: https://www.bonfire.com/store/apophis-shirt-emporium/

Instagrams:
@apophis_enterprises,
@apophisbookemporium,
@apophisscardshop

Twitter: @apophisenterpr1,

Tiktok:@apophisenterprise

Youtube: @sg1fan23477, @FiresideRetreatKingdom

Podcast: Apophis Chat Zone: https://open.spotify.com/show/5zXbrCLEV2xzCp8ybrfHsk?si=fb4d4fdbdce44dec

Newsletter: https://apophiss-newsletter-27c897.beehiiv.com/